TEACHER CONFESSIONS

LAUGHS, LESSONS, *AND THE* ROAD TO ROCK STAR STATUS

TYRA HODGE, Ph.D.

Hodge
PUBLISHING

CONTENTS

INTRODUCTION

Welcome to the wonderfully chaotic world of teaching—a realm filled with laughter, learning, and just a dash of existential dread. In these pages, you're invited to embark on a journey that navigates the highs and lows of being an educator, all while sporting a smile and a willingness to embrace the hilarities that await.

As teachers, we often find ourselves in a unique position: we are somehow expected to juggle the roles of mentor, cheerleader, and therapist, all while maintaining a semblance of professionalism. We walk into our classrooms each day armed with lesson plans, creative strategies, and the hope that today might be the day when our students finally grasp the concept of division (or at least stay awake long enough to give it their best shot).

This book is a celebration of those very moments—the awkward blunders, the victorious breakthroughs, and everything in between. Each chapter presents a humorous yet genuine exploration of various aspects of teaching, from crafting lesson plans that sometimes go hilariously awry to navigating the minefield of classroom feedback. You'll read about the art of creating a classroom environment that feels like a Zen garden (even if it ends up resembling a circus), all while recognizing the power of reflection and self-care in our unpredictable roles.

Unlike traditional educational manuals that focus solely on methods and theory, this book blends playful anecdotes with practical advice. Think of it as a humorous guidebook written by teachers for teachers. When we share our "oops" moments and celebrate our achievements—complete with awards for "Best Unintentional Comedy" and "The 'Oops' Award"—we foster a sense of community, where we can all learn from each other while laughing at our own quirks.

Research shows that reflection and celebration are powerful tools for growth, and as we navigate through this book, you'll find opportunities to think about your own experiences and find humor in them. Ultimately, this journey is about transforming the often-daunting path of teaching into an adventure filled with camaraderie, joy, and plenty of lighthearted reflections.

So grab your favorite pen, find a cozy spot, and get ready to discover the rock star teacher within you. Whether you're a rookie navigating your first year or a seasoned pro looking for a refreshing perspective, this book offers something for everyone. Let's embrace the laughter, tackle the challenges, and celebrate the remarkable journey of being an educator together! Welcome to your confessional, fellow teachers—it's time to turn the page and start this adventure!

CHAPTER ONE

THE RELUCTANT REFLECTION

*Embracing the Dental Dread
of Self-Assessment*

Welcome, dear educators, to the potentially awkward yet oh-so-worthwhile journey of self-assessment! Before you start detecting faint whiffs of dental office antiseptic, let me tell you this: self-evaluation is kind of like going to the dentist. It's uncomfortable, you might dread it, and chances are—just like that probing light in your mouth—there's a lot lurking underneath that we'd rather not examine. Yet, at the end of it all, we walk out feeling lighter, a bit more polished, and with a renewed sense of purpose!

Let's take a moment to think about this comparison. Picture your typical trip to the dentist. You walk in, clutching your coffee-stained teeth with trepidation, praying that the hygienist won't find any unexpected cavities that will lead to extensive drilling. You might even smile nervously, thinking, "I flossed last week, there's no way they'll find any hidden plaque!" But deep down, you know that those occasional checks are crucial for maintaining your dental health.

Well, my friends, self-assessment in teaching works in a remarkably similar way. Sure, it might not have that sterile smell that makes you want to gag (though, I mean, have you smelled a break room after lunch?), but it can sting a little when you realize you've been assigning "light reading" that only consists of cereal boxes and pamphlets about dental hygiene instead of engaging literature. "I thought I was a 'fun' teacher," you might reflect, "but my students turned my 'dance breaks' into a TikTok compilation of the worst moves ever!" Cue the cringeworthy cringe!

Now, let's take a humorous, yet genuine, look at what self-assessment can reveal. When we hold the mirror of self-reflection up to our teaching practices, what do we see? Do we see the shining teeth of success, or the gummy decay of missed opportunities?

Maybe you'll discover that your instructional strategies are as outdated as your middle school mixtape. Remember that time you tried to teach fractions by using pizza slices? Sure, it sounded great in theory, but instead of creating a hands-on learning experience, the kids are just fighting about who gets the biggest slice—because let's be real, they've mastered their negotiation skills way before they've mastered their fractions!

Or perhaps, in your quest to create a warm and engaging atmosphere, you unwittingly transformed your classroom into a chaotic circus. "Why yes, my class sounds exactly like a three-ring circus! Why dance when I can juggle the pain of poor classroom management and the dread of avoiding eye contact with that one kid in the back?" Self-assessment can often bring these hidden truths to light, and that's when the real growth begins.

Being a teacher means you're in the business of shaping minds, but let's not forget—we're also in the business of shaping ourselves. And just like going to the dentist, self-assessment offers a chance to examine the "gums" of our teaching: What's healthy? What's inflamed? What needs a little extra love?

In the upcoming chapters, we're going to dive deep into the nitty-gritty—self-assessment tools, humor-infused reflections, and strategies to polish your teaching strategies just like you'd polish your pearly whites, ("Man, I thought they were shiny before, but wow! Look at them now!"). So grab your coffee, put on your brightest smile (or grimace if you might), and let's embark on this enlightening, and yes, slightly humorous, journey to becoming the best teacher you can be in just one week!

Let this week of self-discovery begin, where you embrace the occasionally uncomfortable reality, dust off your dance moves, and glean those germinating insights hiding beneath the surface. Buckle up—self-assessment doesn't have to be something we dread. After all, who wouldn't want to strut out of this dental examination both healthier and with new tricks up their sleeve?

So, are you ready? Let's take this journey together with a sprinkle of laughter and a hefty dose of revelation. Remember: the only cavities we want are in our chocolate and not in our teaching practice!

Here are a few humorous yet relatable story scenarios for your chapter, "The Reluctant Reflection – Embracing the Dental Dread of Self-Assessment":

SCENARIO 1:
THE GREAT PIZZA FRACTION FIASCO

Last year, I decided to teach fractions using one of the greatest culinary delights known to mankind: pizza. I brought in a large pepperoni pizza, thinking it would be the perfect way to engage my fourth graders. As I divided the pizza into eighths, I asked the students to work out the fractions. However, instead of discussing the math, all my students seemed to care about was who was getting the largest slice. Jack traded his entire snack for a double portion, while Sarah attempted to negotiate adding pineapple to her slice as a bonus.

By the time the lesson ended, we still hadn't covered fractions, but I did gain a new understanding of my students' negotiation skills—and a lesson on why hands-on doesn't always mean productive!

SCENARIO 2:
THE CLASSROOM CIRCUS

In my earnest attempt to create a warm and inviting classroom atmosphere, I inadvertently transformed it into a chaotic circus. One day, as I was trying to implement 'flexible seating' with bean bags and hula hoops, excitement turned into pandemonium. I was juggling lessons, wrangling distracted students, and dodging flying paper airplanes as if I were in a three-ring circus. I realized I had become the ringmaster of chaos rather than a facilitator of learning. During our mid-week self-assessment, I confessed my classroom resembled a 'great escaped zoo' more than a 'place of knowledge,' prompting a hearty laugh from my colleagues, and a much-needed reflection on classroom management strategies.

SCENARIO 3:

DANCE BREAK DISASTERS

As an enthusiastic advocate for integrating movement into my lessons, I scheduled daily "dance breaks" to re-energize my class. One Monday, I confidently led them in a "simple" dance routine, complete with choreography I'd learned from a TikTok video. However, what ensued was a cacophony of flailing arms and off-beat steps. My students turned my well-intentioned break into a hilarious TikTok compilation slated for future embarrassment. Watching their attempts at rhythm, I realized that my eagerness for fun had devolved into a spectacle of chaotic creativity—not exactly the cultural lesson I had hoped for! In the end, the self-reflection revealed the importance of setting clear expectations before initiating what I assumed would be a simple movement break.

SCENARIO 4:

THE ANXIETY OF SELF-ASSESSMENT

I remember my first encounter with self-assessment like it was a dental appointment—anxiety layered with denial. The night before my reflection session, I stayed up late, convincing myself that my students loved every lesson I delivered. Then, when I arrived at the meeting, a colleague innocently asked what I had learned from my students. Suddenly, it hit me: my "engaging" lessons had turned into nothing more than glorified 'sit-and-listen' sessions with a bonus of eye rolls. As I fumbled through explaining my rationalizations, I felt as exposed as I would at the dentist's office! I realized that like dental visits—self-assessments might be uncomfortable, but they provide critical feedback for improvement.

SCENARIO 5:
REFLECTION ON A FIELD TRIP

After a thrilling, yet challenging field trip to a science museum, I took a moment to reflect on the day. My plan was to inspire curiosity about science, but as we attempted to corral twenty hyperactive students into a single exhibit, I was reminded of herding cats. Each time I thought I'd saved a teachable moment, I was quickly guided back to reality by a student who had decided the giant dinosaur skeleton was the perfect backdrop for their upcoming TikTok videos. In my post-trip reflection, I acknowledged that while the day wasn't quite the success I envisioned, it was certainly memorable—and a reminder that flexibility and humor are essential in teaching.

CHAPTER TWO

UNDERSTANDING YOUR STUDENTS

The Secret Lives of Middle Schoolers

Welcome back to the rollercoaster ride of self-improvement! In our quest to become better teachers, we must don our detective hats and dive headfirst into the often baffling world of our students. Because let's face it: understanding middle schoolers can sometimes feel like trying to decode ancient hieroglyphs while solving a Rubik's Cube—blindfolded. They are a curious mix of wild creativity and overwhelming confusion, and they often have secret lives that would put even the best soap operas to shame.

Let's step into the classroom of Mr. Thompson for a moment. Mr. Thompson was your quintessential middle school teacher: a bit frazzled but earnestly trying to connect with his students. One day, as he attempted to lead a discussion about the importance of historical figures, a rather vocal student named Billy declared, "School is a prison!" The class erupted in laughter and nods of agreement, as if Billy had just unveiled a shocking truth about the universe.

"Very well," Mr. Thompson replied, ever the optimist, "if school is a prison, do we get a paper airplane championship as our form of liberation?" And just like that, the air was transformed from dreary lectures on the lives of historical figures to unbridled enthusiasm for crafting the ultimate paper airplane. Billy and his pals turned the classroom into an aviation hub, crafting masterpieces that soared through the air, creating an unexpected camaraderie that united students of all cliques—from the athletes to the bookworms.

This anecdote illustrates a vital truth: sometimes, the most profound connections and engaging learning experiences arise from the quirks and personalities of our students. Understanding who they are—quirks, complaints, and all—can transform a dull lesson into a vibrant exchange. Research has shown that when teachers take the time to understand their students' backgrounds, interests, and unique personalities, it leads to better engagement and academic success. Suddenly, the classroom shifts from a place of mere instruction to a dynamic community where students feel valued and seen.

Now, you might be wondering: "How do I decipher the secret language of my middle schoolers?" Alas, it's not as easy as cracking a simple code. They have their own lexicon—filled with phrases and social nuances that can make your head spin. For instance, while you might think that "lit" refers to something on fire, your students might be using it to describe an excellent time. A lesson that was "lit" is often one that excited them, but who knew it came with a side of fire hazard?

Let's talk about Amanda, a student who created her own social media campaign advocating that teachers should implement "Penguin Day," where everyone dresses like penguins and learns about Antarctica via interpretative dance (trust me, her proposal had some solid research behind it). Amanda's enthusiasm was contagious, and it sparked a series of collaborative projects in which students researched climate change, all while having a good giggle at each other's flailing flippers during their penguin dances.

In both Billy's and Amanda's cases, their antics demonstrated a truth that the academic world often overlooks: when students feel they can express themselves—when their unique personalities and insights are embraced—learning becomes a shared adventure.

However, let's be real for a moment: understanding middle schoolers can sometimes feel like navigating a maze filled with delightful surprises and the occasional unexpected dead end. One minute, they're excited about a project; the next, they're convinced that wearing mismatched socks is a revolutionary statement on individuality. It's downright dizzying!

To better connect with your students, consider the following strategies:

1. Observe and Engage: Take the time to watch how your students interact. What are their interests?

What makes them laugh? Understanding their social dynamics can unlock engagement opportunities.

2. Dare to Ask: Don't shy away from asking your students about their thoughts on topics that matter to them. You might be surprised by their insights. Whether it's TikTok trends or their latest obsessions, showing interest can build bridges.

3. Embrace Humor: Sharing your own quirks—perhaps your terrible dance moves or your love for obscure trivia—can create a sense of relatability. Let's be honest: if you can accidentally turn a lesson into a rant about your latest attempt at baking, your students will likely delight in your earnestness.

4. Collaborative Projects: Like Amanda's "Penguin Day," giving students the chance to propose and lead fun projects fosters a sense of ownership. When they can express their interests, they surprise us with their creativity.

As we journey through this week of introspection and growth, remember: understanding students means embracing their quirks and exploring the secret lives they lead beyond the classroom walls. It's not always an easy task, but it's undoubtedly the most rewarding. With a touch of humor and a willingness to dive deep into their world, we just might discover that these fascinating little creatures—who swear school is a prison one minute and organize plane championships the next—are indeed the key to unlocking a more engaging and lively classroom.

So, grab your magnifying glass and put on your detective cap. Let's decode the delightful mysteries of our students together, and watch as our teaching transforms from drudgery to discovery!

Here are some funny and relatable story scenarios for your chapter, "Understanding Your Students: The Secret Lives of Middle Schoolers":

SCENARIO 1:
THE PAPER AIRPLANE WAR

In a moment of clarity during a particularly convoluted lesson about the Revolutionary War, Mr. Thompson found himself thinking outside the box—or should we say inside the airplane? When Billy declared school a prison, he didn't just spark a conversation; he ignited a full-blown paper airplane war! What started as a bonding experience quickly escalated into chaos as students from across the room began launching their creative designs. The air was filled with the sound of crinkling paper and bursts of laughter. Mr. Thompson watched in disbelief as two rival factions, the "Sky Flyers" and the "Aviators," emerged. Soon, students were wearing makeshift pilot goggles fashioned out of stapled paper and taking their positions for battle. All while Mr. Thompson struggled to regain control, suspecting this might be the most engaging lesson he'd had all year—or the most effective distraction from the actual curriculum!

SCENARIO 2:

THE "LIT" LANGUAGE BARRIER

During a class discussion that quickly turned into a vocabulary lesson, Mr. Thompson noticed a few puzzled looks when he asked the students what they thought about the new historical documentary. "Wasn't it lit?" he ventured. The students erupted into hysterics, leaving Mr. Thompson baffled. "Yeah, Mr. T, if by 'lit' you mean 'boring as watching paint dry!'" suggested Jamie. This prompted a class-wide debate over words that had completely new meanings: "Why do you think they call it 'lit' when we're the ones who are supposed to be on fire with excitement?" asked Maria, as she dramatically fanned her non-existent flames. The entire class was in stitches by the end, and Mr. Thompson made a mental note to brush up on middle school lingo, because clearly, he was living in 1995!

SCENARIO 3:

AMANDA'S PENGUIN PROPOSAL

When Amanda waltzed into class sporting a tuxedo t-shirt and carrying a stuffed penguin, Mr. Thompson knew he was in for an imaginative day. Unlike any conventional project, Amanda passionately pitched her idea for "Penguin Day"—a day dedicated to dressing like penguins while incorporating interpretive dance into every subject. "It's climate education combined with fabulous fashion!" she exclaimed. Enthralled by her enthusiasm, Mr. Thompson let her lead the charge, and the school staff watched in bewilderment as the entire grade shuffled into the cafeteria, wiggling their "flippers" while trying to answer trivia questions about Antarctica. Amanda's presentation quickly turned into an impromptu TikTok sensation. As the videos racked up views online, Mr. Thompson couldn't help but think: talk about a lesson on global warming taking the world by storm!

SCENARIO 4:
THE SOCK REVOLUTION

A typical Wednesday turned into a spectacle when, prompted by a random online video, Jonah convinced the class that mismatched socks symbolized their unique individuality. What began as one student's fashion statement snowballed into an all-out "Mismatched Sock Day" at school. Suddenly, Mr. Thompson's classroom looked like a refugee camp for laundry disasters—bright pink socks paired with neon green stripes, polka dots fighting for space against plaid. "No one can tell me what to do!" Jonah declared, brandishing his outrageous mismatched ensemble. Mr. Thompson couldn't contain his laughter as he joined in sporting his own funkiest sock combo, realizing that humor not only broke the ice but also transformed a mundane Wednesday into a vibrant expression of creativity. And hey, sometimes the best history lessons come when students choose to express themselves—even if it starts in their sock drawer!

SCENARIO 5:
THE TIKTOK RANT

One day, in a fit of creative inspiration, Mr. Thompson decided to bring in a random hobby to share with his students—baking. "Let's bake a cake to teach measurements and fractions!" he exclaimed, as the students exchanged skeptical glances. Halfway through the baking demonstration, he accidentally mixed up teaspoons and tablespoons, resulting in what can only be described as a "volcano of cake batter." As chaos ensued, a student started a TikTok live stream titled "Mr. T's Baking Fiasco." Mr. Thompson went from terrible teacher to TikTok star as the video racked up views of him trying to save his cake while simultaneously incorporating math lessons. The students were thrilled, and suddenly, Mr. Thompson became the "Baking Teacher"—completely eclipsing his historical persona. Lesson learned: sometimes, a baking blunder is all it takes to engage students in unexpected ways.

CHAPTER THREE

LESSON PLANNING

*When You Plan to Fail, You
Actually Succeed*

Welcome to the circus, folks! Step right up and witness the chaotic wonders of lesson planning! As seasoned educators know, planning is supposed to lay the groundwork for successful lessons, yet sometimes it feels more like juggling flaming torches while riding a unicycle on a tightrope. In this chapter, we'll dive into the art of lesson planning, complete with hilarious mishaps that remind us that failure can sometimes be our greatest teacher —even when it sets off a mini eruption of baking soda volcanoes.

Let's start with the humble volcano experiment—a classic teaching staple. Picture this: a group of enthusiastic fourth graders, eagerly awaiting the chance to watch the magic of science unfold. Mrs. Jenkins, a well-intentioned teacher, spent the weekend meticulously planning her lesson. She prepared the perfect mix of vinegar and baking soda, excited to demonstrate a chemical reaction that would wow her students. However, amidst the excitement, she miscalculated the amounts and ended up with a concoction reminiscent of an explosive adventure!

As the class gathered around the volcano made of paper-mâché, Mrs. Jenkins proudly added vinegar to the baking soda. With a dramatic flourish, she exclaimed, "Here we go!" Instead of a gentle bubbling, a veritable geyser erupted, sending a foamy cascade of baking soda and vinegar shooting across the classroom! It foamed over the sides, coating the front rows of astonished students. "It's a scientific eruption!" she declared, trying to maintain her composure as the kids erupted into laughter. The cleanup took longer than the experimentation itself, but guess what? Students remembered that lesson like it was the most exciting theme park ride.

Research shows that while lesson planning is essential, flexibility is equally important. A rigid plan can quickly turn into a locked vault when students need to pivot or when the world itself throws a curveball—like the volcano explosion! When we allow our lessons to flow organically, we create an environment that fosters creativity, excitement, and engagement.

Let's not forget about the group presentations. In an attempt to integrate fun and creativity into her history lesson, Ms. Rodriguez decided to have her students present their projects as rap battles. She thought: "What a modern way to engage students!" However, as the day approached and the students started to script their presentations, things took an unexpected turn.

On presentation day, instead of presenting their research on historical figures through structured rap songs, the class devolved into an all-out rap battle tournament. There was shouting, beatboxing, and surprisingly intense lyrical exchanges about George Washington's wooden teeth versus Thomas Jefferson's love for all things French. One student even tossed in a spontaneous dance break mid-verse, which resulted in a classroom mosh pit.

While Ms. Rodriguez initially panicked, she eventually realized that the students were actively engaging with the material in a way she never imagined. The chaos transformed into a vibrant energy that solidified their understanding of history. That day, they weren't just reciting facts; they were immersing themselves in the narrative, and the smiles on their faces were brighter than any textbook could evoke.

This brings us to one of the most important lessons about flexible planning: it sometimes feels like trying to master circus tricks. You might feel like you're about to drop the flaming baton, and instead, you find a way to spin it into a graceful performance. Flexibility allows us to adapt and capitalize on those glorious moments of spontaneity that can lead our lessons in unexpected yet fruitful directions.

To embrace this type of planning, consider the following tips:

1. Plan with Possibilities: Leave room in your lesson for spontaneous discussions or activities.

Rather than rigidly adhering to every detail, allow for organic conversation and exploration. An "oops" moment can often turn into a "wow!" moment.

2. Have Backup Activities: Equip yourself with a few fun activities that can serve as diversions or enhancements, just in case your original plan veers off course. Did the volcano experiment fail? Break out the art supplies for an impromptu design-a-volcano contest!

3. Ease into Flexibility: Start small—test the waters with a few lessons where you encourage students to take charge. Let them steer the ship occasionally—or at least call out the destinations!

4. Embrace the Unplanned: Not every lesson needs to be a well-oiled machine. Sometimes, the scattered chaos of students' creativity and excitement can yield the most unforgettable learning experiences—even if it means the occasional baking soda eruption!

As we navigate through our week of discovery and improvement, remember that good lesson plans can lead to great outcomes, but the best learning happens when we embrace the unexpected. After all, planning to fail sometimes leads to a symphony of laughter, creativity, and authentic learning experiences. So, next time you find yourself in a whirl of chaos amidst your perfectly drawn plans, take a deep breath and remember: in the world of teaching, flexibility is the ultimate skill—and sometimes, your greatest educational triumphs arise from delightful chaos.

Here are some funny and relatable story scenarios for your chapter, "Lesson Planning: When You Plan to Fail, You Actually Succeed":

SCENARIO 1:
THE GREAT BAKING SODA ERUPTION

Mrs. Jenkins had every intention of delivering a spectacular science lesson on chemical reactions with her baking soda volcano. She practiced measuring out vinegar and baking soda at home, envisioning a perfectly controlled eruption. Alas, on the big day, her excitement led to an overzealous pouring that sent an explosive plume of frothy mixture cascading over the edges of the volcano! The first few rows of students were caught in the splash zone, covered in sticky baking soda goo as they squealed with laughter. "It's a scientific eruption!" Mrs. Jenkins announced, channeling her inner game show host while frantically grabbing paper towels. The students left the class declaring it the most epic lesson ever, and Mrs. Jenkins learned that sometimes, the best lessons come with an unexpected mess and a lot of giggles.

SCENARIO 2:
THE RAP BATTLE ROYALE

Ms. Rodriguez thought she had a brilliant lesson planned when she introduced rap battles to cover historical figures. She imagined students delivering insightful verses about their topics, but what really happened felt more like an episode of a quirky reality show. When the students took the stage, the classroom erupted into a full-blown "Rap Battle Royale." "Yo, George Washington with my wooden teeth, I'll outshine you from head to feet!" one student rhymed, while another dropped a beat that had classmates bouncing in their seats. There were wild dance breaks, passionate arguments about who had the best signature, and even an impromptu debate on who made the better French fries—Jefferson or Lincoln. The lyrical genius may have been a bit questionable, but the enthusiasm was off the charts, proving that sometimes lessons evolve into unexpected masterpieces of hilarity and engagement!

SCENARIO 3:
MATH CLASS GONE WILD

Mr. Thompson had meticulously planned a math lesson focused on fractions, aiming for a smooth explanation and practice time. However, when he announced an interactive game where students would "divide" a pizza (made of foam, of course), the classroom erupted in a frenzy of competitive spirit. Instead of calmly discussing fractions, students began bartering pieces of foam pizza like it was a black market. "I'll give you two slices for the pepperoni one!" shouted one student while others scrambled to create the largest imaginary pizza party possible. At first,

Mr. Thompson thought he had lost control of the lesson until he realized they learned more about fractions through their enthusiastic (and slightly chaotic) negotiations than he could have ever taught from the board. Dazed but impressed, he joined the fun, declaring, "I guess we're all dividing and conquering today!"

SCENARIO 4:
THE DAY ART TOOK OVER SCIENCE

During a units planning meeting, Ms. Jenkins decided to mix art into her science curriculum. Alarm bells should have gone off when she suggested the students create models of cells using marshmallows, but excitement ruled the day. When the project commenced, half the class turned into an art studio filled with edible cell models, while the other half attempted to stage an intense marshmallow food fight. With gooey marshmallows smeared across faces and walls, Ms. Jenkins tried to maintain some semblance of order. "Remember, this is science, not a culinary circus!" she laughed, waving a gummy bear as if it were an authoritative pointer.

Ultimately, the lesson transformed into a memorable and sticky experience where students learned more about cell structure from the chaos than they ever would have from the textbook!

SCENARIO 5:

THE SPONTANEOUS CREATIVITY CHALLENGE

In a fit of inspiration, Ms. Rodriguez decided to hold a spontaneous "Creativity Challenge" during her lesson. "Okay, everyone, instead of presenting your projects, let's come up with a completely new way to teach this topic!" she announced, reveling in the surprise that lit up students' faces. What followed was a nonsensical whirlwind of ideas: one student proposed performing a skit about the agricultural revolution involving farm animals (with sock puppets made from actual socks), while another suggested reenacting the signing of the Declaration of Independence with silly costumes. As the classroom erupted into chaotic brainstorming, Ms. Rodriguez couldn't help but smile. The lesson devolved into delightful chaos, but the students learned from each other and ended up creating a mashup of performances so entertaining that even the custodian had to peek in, laughing at the hilarity, and the principal later remarked it was one of the best displays of student engagement he'd seen all year!

CHAPTER FOUR

ENGAGING TECHNIQUES

*How to Keep Them Awake
Without Coffee*

Welcome back, fearless educators! If you're reading this chapter, it's likely because you're on a mission to discover the magical formula for keeping your students awake and engaged without resorting to the potent wizardry of caffeine. Let's face it: sometimes, teaching feels like trying to rally a group of hibernating bears—particularly in those post-lunch, pre-recess moments when eyelids droop and attention spans vanish quicker than a good donut in the teacher's lounge.

To tackle this challenge, many teachers have resorted to some of the most creative (and often humorous) techniques to engage their students. Ready? Here we go!

First up: the Dance-Off for Answers. Picture this scene: Mrs. Thompson, faced with a group of lethargic seventh graders sliding into the land of catnaps, decides it's time to introduce a little movement into her lesson on algebraic equations. She declares, "Alright, kids! Before you answer the next question, let's see your best dance moves!" Suddenly, the classroom transforms into a dance floor, and students are twirling, shuffling, and attempting very questionable robot moves for the privilege of answering a math problem.

Not only does this technique get the blood pumping, but it also leads to delighted giggles and enthusiastic participation. Who knew that breaking a sweat could clarify the difference between 'x' and 'why can't I just add cotton candy instead?' Unfortunately, the aftermath often includes a disaster zone of scattered belongings, but hey, you can't blame a teacher for trying to mix fun with learning, right?

And let's talk about surprise pop quizzes. Now, these delightful little beasts often float under the guise of "assessments," but let's be honest, they sometimes feel more like an episode of a game show—complete with nerve-racking music and dramatic pauses. "Will Billy make the grade, or will he leave us gasping for the right answer?" When Mr. Lee pulls out the infamous quiz cards, you can almost hear the students whispering their collective prayers to the quiz gods. Sometimes, in the heat of the moment, rather than going for accuracy, they'll throw out answers that come straight from the depths of the random knowledge abyss.

"Who was the first president?" "Uhhh, George Washington?" "What's the capital of France?" "Eiffel Tower!" Pro tip: if you ever find yourself in a teaching rut, just throw in a pop quiz with wild stakes—maybe the winner gets to pick the next class movie. It turns even the most mundane of questions into high-stakes game show fun.

Research has shown that student engagement is crucial for an effective learning environment. Engaged students pay better attention, retain information more efficiently, and overall, have a more positive attitude towards their education. All this sounds great in theory, but in practice, there are days when it feels like you're just one corny joke away from utter classroom silence. Those moments where you think, "Maybe 'Why did the math book look so sad? Because it had too many problems!' was not the crowd-pleaser I predicted…"

Sure, some students snicker at your dad jokes, while others stare blankly, wondering if there's a global shortage of decent punchlines. But here's the kicker: even when the punchlines flop, the effort plants the seeds of connection. It shows students that you're willing to be silly and relatable, and in turn, they're often more likely to reciprocate with lively participation.

Here are some engaging techniques to keep your class alert and alive—minus the coffee:

1. Gamify Lessons: Add gameplay elements to your teaching. Think of quizzes as games, and introduce point systems, badges, or goofy prizes. No one can resist the allure of victory, especially with a trophy that looks like a giant pencil!

2. Incorporate Technology: Use tools like Kahoot! or Quizizz to turn assessments into interactive experiences. Students practically bounce out of their seats when answering questions on their devices, and the instant feedback makes learning feel dynamic.

3. Movement Breaks: Integrate short, energetic breaks throughout the lesson—think a quick round of charades or stretching like a pretzel. It revitalizes attention and sends students back to their seats ready to absorb more knowledge.

4. Creative Group Work: Instead of traditional group projects, let students collaborate in unexpected ways. Encourage them to create skits, puppet shows, or even improv comedy routines about subject material. Trust me, nothing wakes them up faster than the thought of becoming the next dramatic star.

5. Student-Led Lessons: Give students the spotlight and empower them to teach their classmates about topics they're passionate about. Not only does this engage their interests, but it often

leads to unexpected and funny presentations that keep everyone on their toes.

As you work through this chapter, remember to embrace the laughter, the surprises, and the wonderfully unpredictable energy that your students bring. While we may not possess the magic potion for keeping them awake, we certainly have the creativity, passion, and humor to make every lesson an adventure.

So, load up on your corniest jokes and prepare for more unexpected dance-offs! After all, engaging techniques might just be your secret weapon as you journey toward becoming an even better teacher. Let's swing into the next chapter, where we tackle the fine art of classroom management—because keeping the circus running smoothly is a whole different ballgame!

· Here are some funny and engaging story scenarios for your chapter, "Engaging Techniques: How to Keep Them Awake Without Coffee":

SCENARIO 1:

MRS. THOMPSON'S DANCE-OFF DILEMMA

When the afternoon slump hit hard, Mrs. Thompson knew she had to take action. Instead of letting her seventh graders fade into the land of daydreams, she announced a surprise Dance-Off for Answers. The rules were simple: answer a math question, then show off your best dance move.

As the first problem was posed, students started moving like a mix between seasoned dancers and awkward robots trying to figure out their first steps. "Who can solve for x while doing the worm?" she challenged. The class erupted into laughter as Carlos attempted a breakdancing spin until he accidentally knocked over a chair, sending him crashing to the floor—but not before delivering the answer amidst giggles.

By the end of the class, not only had they solved their equations, but Mrs. Thompson had also learned that her classroom could double as a dance studio—albeit a very messy one. Who knew algebra could turn into an impromptu dance party?

GAME SHOW POP QUIZZES

In a bid to revitalize the spirit of inquiry, Mr. Lee decided to turn his pop quizzes into full-blown game shows. "Welcome to Quizmaster's Challenge!" he announced, sporting a glittery bow tie and oversized glasses. Students chuckled as he flipped a giant cardboard arrow that spun to reveal the category: History!

As soon as he pulled out the infamous quiz cards, the room turned electric. "Who was the first president?" he asked. "Uhhh, Ellen DeGeneres?" one student blurted out in a fit of giggles. "Great guess, but the answer is—George Washington!" the teacher responded, quickly adding, "And I expect no one to call you out for confusing the two at their next trivia night!"

As the quiz progressed, answers ranged from the utterly ridiculous to the surprisingly insightful, like one student declaring France's capital as "Eiffel Tower" and somehow defending it with passionate reasoning. The sheer creativity around incorrect answers became the highlight of the class. By the end, Mr. Lee decided that maybe he'd mix in a few more game shows—after all, who wouldn't want to crown a trivia champion by the end of the week?

SCENARIO 3:

THE DAD JOKE COMPETITION

Thinking he was the king of corny puns; Mr. Smith decided it was time to engage his students with a Dad Joke Challenge. "Alright, who can make the class laugh the hardest?" he asked, as the room filled with bemused stares. "Why did the scarecrow win an award? Because he was outstanding in his field!"

The laughter was tepid at best, but Mr. Smith forged ahead. "Okay, tougher crowd! Why did the math book look sad? Because it had too many problems!" At this point, the students were shaking their heads and groaning in the protective manner of teenagers.

Realizing he needed to pivot, he declared, "Alright, your turn! Best pun wins a free homework pass!" Suddenly, students began firing off knock-knock jokes, riddles, and even a few questionable one-liners. Not only did this break the tension, but it also reminded Mr. Smith that humor—even when punctuated with groans—brought some warmth and connection to the room.

SCENARIO 4:

MOVEMENT MAYHEM

In the midst of a long history lesson, Ms. Johnson remembered her "Movement Break" technique. "Alright, everyone! Time for the history hustle!" she declared, leading the students into a quick game of charades where they had to act out historical figures.

Chaos erupted as students tried to mime Julius Caesar being stabbed by Brutus, while another group wrestled with how to express Rosie the Riveter. The class quickly devolved into fits of laughter as students leaped, mimicked, and ad-libbed.

Just when Ms. Johnson thought they had lost track of history entirely, she paused to listen to one student's enthusiastic attempt at explaining the English Civil War through interpretative dance. "What's this? We're now pioneers in historical performance art!" she exclaimed, fully embracing the silliness. By the end, the students not only got a workout but a hilarious perspective on the past—and Ms. Johnson realized authentic learning often has its own energetic rhythm.

SCENARIO 5:

THE STUDENT-LED SPECTACULAR

When Ms. Garcia decided to have students present their research topics, she unleashed a wave of creativity she hadn't anticipated. "You guys can choose any format!" she said, expecting PowerPoint slides and posters. Instead, she was treated to a dazzling array of performances: skits, rap songs, and even a pop quiz where students dressed as historical figures and argued over the merits of Thomas Edison versus Nikola Tesla in a talk-show format.

"Why invent a lightbulb when you can wrestle with a current?" quipped one student in a makeshift wrestling outfit, and to everyone's surprise, the class erupted into raucous cheers. The unexpected humor transformed the lesson, and for the rest of the day, the classroom buzzed with excitement and laughter. Ms. Garcia couldn't help but feel like a proud director of a chaotic show, launching the students into an educational experience they wouldn't soon forget.

CHAPTER FIVE

FEEDBACK

*Playing the Role of a Teacher
and a Therapist*

Ah, feedback: the delicate dance that every teacher must master, often requiring one part teacherly guidance and one part therapist-level empathy. In this chapter, we'll explore the intricacies of offering constructive criticism without causing existential crises in our young scholars, all while maintaining the appearance of someone who just handed out gold stars and snacks.

Imagine this scenario: you sit down to review a stack of essays, your keen eye scanning each word like a hawk. You come across Jason's assignment about existential dread—the kind of essay that makes you question your very existence while simultaneously wondering if he could have written it while lying on a therapist's couch. As you prepare your feedback, he pops his head up and innocently asks, "Did I... um, pass?"

At that moment, you feel the weight of the world on your shoulders. How do you deliver feedback while simultaneously reassuring him that no, he's not doomed to fail in life just because he couldn't fully articulate his concepts? If only you could respond with a confident grin and say, "Absolutely! You made great contributions to the nuances of despair!" instead of, "Well, Jason, let's address the fact that I hadn't realized I signed up to assess a midterm in 'Philosophy of Life' instead of high school English."

This juxtaposition of roles—the kindly teacher and the supportive therapist—often creates an ironic tension. On one hand, you want to encourage your students, and on the other, you must deliver feedback that is honest and constructive. It can feel like a high-wire act where one wrong word sends a student into a philosophical spiral, and you're left wondering if you should whip out a gold star for effort or just the "I survived teaching" sticker.

Research consistently emphasizes the power of feedback. Studies show that constructive criticism can significantly improve student performance by providing clarity and direction. Yet, the irony remains: delivering this feedback while keeping a balanced smile feels almost acrobatic. You know how vital it is, yet each encounter sometimes feels like you're navigating a minefield.

Consider the case of Sarah, who turned in a science project about black holes. As you praise her for the creative presentation, she interjects, "So, you think it's good enough to show at the science fair?" Here lies the moment fraught with possibility and peril! "Well, it has potential, but let's talk about the small issue of it being entirely in comic sans." You can see the light in her eyes dim over the mention of font choice, and suddenly you feel like the villain in a superhero movie, responsible for crushing her dreams. But fear not! You can soften the blow with humor. "Think of comic sans as the mullet of fonts: business up front, party in the back... and just not appropriate for a black hole!"

Navigating feedback, especially with humor, is essential because it not only lightens the mood but also fosters an environment where students feel safe to ask questions. Here are a few tips to maintain that delicate balance between critique and encouragement:

1. Begin with Positives: Start your feedback sessions with what the student did well. "Wow, you have a great grasp of the concept! Now let's talk about how to turn existential dread into a coherent thesis statement."

2. Be Relatable: Share your own "oops" moments, where your feedback led to unexpected realizations. Let them know that everyone—yes, even teachers—has faced their own black holes of confusion!

3. Encourage Dialogue: Make feedback a two-way conversation. Instead of just presenting your thoughts, ask them what they think about their work. "How do you feel about your argument on why the universe is just a figment of our collective imagination?"

4. Use Humor Wisely: A well-timed joke or a gentle tease can defuse any tense situation. If a paper's analysis reads like something out of a horror movie, you might say, "This is so intense, I might need a therapist after reading this!"

5. Frame Feedback as a Growth Opportunity: Shift the perspective from "You need to fix this" to "Here's how you can make your awesome work even better!" Feedback should be seen as a steppingstone rather than a stumbling block.

As we continue our journey through becoming better educators, remember that mastering the art of feedback is a skill that not only helps your students grow but can also make you grow alongside them. You're not just a teacher—you're a guide on a trip where existential dread sometimes raises its head, and a good sense of humor can keep the spirits (and engagement) high.

So, grab your metaphorical tightrope and get ready for your next performance, because providing feedback is just as much about the student's success as it is about keeping your own sanity in check! The act of weaving through constructive criticism can lead to enlightening conversations and ultimately stronger bonds between you and your students.

SCENARIO 1:
THE EXISTENTIAL DREAD ESSAY

After hours of grading, you come across Jason's essay on existential dread—complete with references to his favorite philosophers and the occasional line that leaves you pondering your own life choices. As he leans in with big, hopeful eyes, he asks, "Did I pass?" You take a breath, reminding yourself not to crush his spirits.

"Absolutely, Jason! Your essay beautifully explores the meaning of life—and by the way, it's deep enough to require flotation devices," you say with a smile, teasing him gently. "However, we might need to work on clarity; I'm not sure if you were arguing for or against the concept of existence." He looks puzzled but relieved, and you think, "Phew! I didn't send him spiraling into a full-on midlife crisis!"

SCENARIO 2:

THE COMIC SANS CRISIS

Sarah presents her black hole science project proudly, only for you to pause mid-praise as you notice it's entirely in Comic Sans. "Great creativity, Sarah! But, um, let's discuss your font choice," you say cautiously. "Comic Sans is like wearing Crocs to a formal wedding—innovative, but maybe not the best fit for the theme." Sarah's face falls a little, but you can't resist adding, "Think of it this way: You can have fun at the wedding in your Crocs, but for black holes, let's aim for something a bit more... universal!"

As she chuckles at the analogy, you both brainstorm more appropriate fonts together. The moment lightens, and you realize that turning the feedback into a moment of collaboration creates a more comfortable learning environment.

SCENARIO 3:

THE FEEDBACK TANGO

While reviewing Carlos's paper about the water cycle, you notice several factual inaccuracies. As you sit down with him, he confidently asks, "Was it an A-plus paper?" You take a deep breath, feeling like you're about to tiptoe through a minefield. "Well, Carlos, let's say this paper swam beautifully through the water cycle—until it hit a waterfall!"

His eyes widen with confusion. "A waterfall?"

"Yes! While the concept was great, a few facts crashed down unexpectedly. But fear not! This is just a bump in your academic journey, and we can work together to get you back on solid ground," you assure him. He perks up, realizing that each 'waterfall' is just another lesson towards mastering the art of water!

SCENARIO 4:
THE HORROR MOVIE CRITIQUE

Stacey hands in an essay that reads like a horror movie script, complete with tension-building phrases and cliffhanger endings. "This is intense, Stacey! I almost waited for the monster to leap off the page!" you exclaim, trying to gauge her reaction. Instead of rolling her eyes, she giggles and grins, clearly appreciating the absurdity.

You continue, "But, let's think about what makes a good thesis stronger, just like how we wouldn't want a horror film to end with 'And then everyone was scared forever'—let's give it a more definitive ending!" The blend of humor and genuine critique unlocks an engaging discussion on storytelling, and you leave with a humorous anecdote about how her essay might haunt your dreams for weeks!

SCENARIO 5:
THE PHILOSOPHICAL DEBATE

While discussing feedback in class, you turn to a particularly tumultuous essay by Derek, who questioned the very fabric of reality. "Derek, your essay was quite thought-provoking—like if Aristotle and a cat on a keyboard collaborated!" His eyes shine with uncertainty, so you lean in, "But among the esoteric musings, this section about why cats are actually aliens might need a little more backing."

He looks puzzled, so with a sly grin, you add, "Let's channel your existential pondering into a more structured argument. After all, even if cats are aliens, we need evidence to convince everyone else!"

Through laughter and playful banter, you guide him through refining his arguments while showing that feedback can be enlightening and enjoyable—after all, who wouldn't want to debate the alien origins of cats?

In the next chapter, we will tackle the often-overlooked realm of self-care for teachers. Don't worry—we'll dive into ways to keep you energized and ready to face the labyrinth of academia!

CHAPTER SIX

CLASSROOM ENVIRONMENT

From Chaos to a Zen Garden (Almost)

Ah, the classroom environment—the sacred space where learning happens, dreams are nurtured, and chaos reigns supreme! In this chapter, we'll explore how to cultivate a positive atmosphere that feels like a tranquil Zen garden, even if it often resembles a three-ring circus filled with juggling clowns, acrobatics, and the occasional lion roaring for attention.

Creating this serene sanctuary often starts with the concept of classroom decor. Imagine, if you will, transforming your chaotic classroom into an oasis of calm, with soothing colors, whimsical quotes, and a few strategically placed plants that you hope the students won't accidentally turn into modern art installations. Yes, we're aiming for a Zen garden aesthetic here—where everything feels balanced and serene—rather than a backdrop for a "Survivor: Middle School Edition" reality show.

Let's talk about those plants, shall we? Every year, you diligently select a few green friends to grace your classroom. You envision a harmonious space where students' minds can bloom alongside their leafy companions. However, there's an unspoken rule that middle schoolers and plants simply do not mix. The plants, of course, do not get watered; they become living tributes to neglect. One week, they're vibrant and lush, the next they are drooping like sad little green flags of surrender. But hey, at least they offer a wonderful contrast to the chaos of textbooks and scattered papers that dominate the desks!

Speaking of chaos, let's not forget the Herculean effort it takes to maintain some semblance of order. Picture this: you stand at the front of the classroom, voice steady, as you repeat, "No phones during class!" Yet, there they are, like moths to a flame—students stealthily texting under their desks, desperately trying to look engaged while their gazes flicker downwards. It often feels like you're trying to reign in a pack of hyper puppies at the park. "Look! A squirrel!"—only instead of squirrels, it's TikTok videos that draw your students' attention away.

Research indicates that a positive classroom environment significantly enhances student learning experiences, but managing this environment can often feel like performing a magic trick on a tightrope. You might feel like you're juggling the needs of your students while simultaneously dodging their various distractions. The ideal atmosphere is calm and welcoming, yet the daily reality resembles a colorful circus where student personalities clash in amusing ways.

To build that ideal environment (or something close enough), consider these tips sprinkled with a touch of humor:

1. Create a Cozy Corner: Designate a spot in your classroom where students can retreat when they

need a moment to breathe. This corner can have bean bags, soft pillows, and perhaps a sign that says, "Welcome to your inner Zen." Just be ready for someone to camp out there permanently!

2. Utilize Visual Aids: Use colorful charts, inspirational quotes, and student artwork to create a vibrant, engaging space. Just remember, if you turn the posters into a paper airplane contest, all those positive vibes may get rearranged!

3. Set Clear Expectations: It's essential to establish rules about behavior that foster respect and calm. Think of your classroom guidelines like a beautiful landscape, where everything has its place. "No phones" should be as clear as "no stepping on the flower beds!"

4. Interactive Learning Stations: Create different zones in your classroom for various types of lessons (reading nook, math zone, art corner). Each zone can have decorated signs with catchy names—like "The Reading Rainforest"—to draw students in. Unfortunately, every rainforest also has its storms!

5. Incorporate Mindfulness Moments: Integrate short breaks for mindfulness, like closing eyes and visualizing a peaceful scene—perhaps one without sticky notes stuck to shoes and back-packs. But beware: their imaginations may drift to daydreams about lunch or the basketball game after school!

6. Encourage Ownership: Give students roles in maintaining the order and beauty of the class-room. Perhaps they can take turns watering the plants or tidying up. Just remember, the last student tasked with watering them might just come back with a green thumb and the plants may end up in a flourishing fashion show... or completely wilted.

As we navigate the realities of creating our ideal class-room environment, let's remember that aiming for a tranquil space doesn't mean that chaos won't find its way in. Even amid the chaos, we can find laughter and resilience, weaving together the fun of discovery with the beauty of learning.

The truth is, establishing a Zen garden in the middle of a vibrant middle school often mirrors the experience of cultivating a delightful mess. It requires patience, creativity, and a hearty sense of humor. As we look to foster a space that promotes positivity and growth, let's giggle at the chaos, embrace the mishaps, and appreciate the small victories in our circus of learning.

Here are some funny and engaging story scenarios for your chapter, "Classroom Environment: From Chaos to a Zen Garden (Almost)":

SCENARIO 1:
THE BOTANICAL CATASTROPHE

Every fall, you excitedly bring in a selection of plants to create your tranquil classroom oasis. You envision bright green ferns and cheerful flowers breathing life into the space. However, by the end of week one, your new botanical buddies look more like the backdrop to a horror movie than the peaceful garden you intended.

One day, as you scan the room, you catch a group of students staring at your once-thriving plant that has drastically wilted. "Hey, the plant looks a bit… under the weather," you joke. "Did anybody offer it a glass of water or maybe a pep talk?"

A student pipes up, "It's just embracing its inner zen! It's meditating!"

"Well, let's channel that zen energy into actual water instead!" you suggest cheerfully. Two days later, despite the collective student effort to revitalize the plant, it remains a sad green lump. You decide that perhaps plastic plants are the way to go—at least they won't mind the neglect... or turn your classroom into a floral graveyard!

SCENARIO 2:
THE PHONE WARS

You face off against a battalion of distracted students, smartphones hidden at their desks like prized possessions. "Alright, class! Phones away! This isn't a music festival; it's math time!" you boldly declare. But just as you say that, a faint sound drifts through the air: a catchy TikTok dance clip.

"Is that a phone I hear?" you ask, squinting suspiciously at Jason in the back. He shoots a sheepish grin, trying to look completely innocent. "I swear I heard a squirrel," he replies, making wild gesticulations as if to distract you.

"Oh, you heard a squirrel, huh? Is that how you refer to your phone now?" you fire back, suppressing laughter. As you enact a dramatic, mock-serious crackdown on the phones, the class bursts into fits of giggles. Maybe it's time to set up a "phone jail" where they can meet their "sentence" during class—five minutes of focusing without their beloved devices.

SCENARIO 3:

THE COZY CORNER SAGA

After negotiating a "Cozy Corner" in your classroom—a place where students can retreat with soft pillows and bean bags—you expect it to be a calming space. You even put up a sign that says, "Welcome to Your Inner Zen."

However, within days, it transforms into an impromptu hangout spot; suddenly, students are staging pillow forts and organizing nap times. One of them turns to you and earnestly asks, "Can we change the sign to 'Welcome to Your Inner Nap Zone'?"

You sigh and chuckle. "Well, as long as you can demonstrate the differences between sleeping and learning, I suppose that's fine! But just remember, those are not the same zones!" You watch them roll their eyes and settle into their forts, embracing this new "educational" definition of relaxation.

SCENARIO 4:
THE INTERACTIVE LEARNING STATIONS

Excited about setting up different learning stations, you create themed zones like "The Reading Rainforest" and "The Math Mountain." Each area has catchy decorations and vibrant signs to draw students in.

Yet, on the first day of rotation, chaos ensues as students charge from station to station, treating your thoughtful setup more like an amusement park than an educational experience. You peer into "The Math Mountain," where a group of students has turned math problems into a competitive sport, calculating scores as if it's the most exhilarating game show in history.

They're bouncing off the walls while furiously shouting mathematical formulas.

"Usually the math mountain is supposed to be a calm place, much like actual mountains!" they exclaim, still buzzing with energy from their newfound madness.

You can't help but laugh and think, "Well, there goes my idea of a tranquil learning environment!" Time to recalibrate those stations—and maybe add some soft "mountain" sounds in the background!

SCENARIO 5:

MINDFULNESS MOMENTS GONE AWRY

You decide to introduce mindfulness moments to ground the class, instructing them to close their eyes and imagine a tranquil beach. However, as you guide them through visualization, you suddenly catch a student snoring softly.

Realizing the peaceful beach has morphed into a snooze fest, you gently remind them, "Hey, this is a mindfulness moment, not a 'nap time on the beach' moment!"

A skeptical student opens one eye and deadpans, "But this is just, like, a beach in winter, right? Who wants to be awake in January?" The room erupts in laughter, and instead of a zen session, you're suddenly discussing beach vacation plans.

It seems that your mindfulness moments may need a little extra energy—perhaps some ocean wave sounds... or maybe just less actual relaxation.

These scenarios highlight the humorous and chaotic nature of creating an ideal classroom environment. They illustrate the challenges educators face while striving for an atmosphere conducive to learning—all while trying to navigate the unpredictability that middle schoolers bring along with their boundless energy.

And as we segue into our next chapter, hold tight! It's time to tackle the essential topic of student motivation —you know, the elusive and often confounding force that can propel or derail even the best-laid plans!

CHAPTER 7

REFLECTION

The Teacher's Confessional

Welcome, weary educators, to the Sanctuary of Reflection—better known as the "teacher confessional." Here, we can openly uproot our funny grievances, share our proud moments, and maybe even laugh a little at ourselves. Just like any good confession, this might be awkward at first, but the healing power of humor and reflection is what we need to emerge stronger in our teaching journeys.

Let's take a moment to step into the confessional booth together. Picture it: candlelight (or maybe your flickering overhead classroom lights), shelves lined with motivational posters that basically say, "You've got this!" and a comfy chair—okay, let's be honest, it's just your desk chair with some extra cushions you snagged from the lounge.

Here's a classic example: remember that time you were attempting to explain the concept of "general" in an English lesson and ended up accidentally saying "genital"? The gasps emanating from the students could have rivaled the dramatic pause in a horror movie. "Today, we're going to discuss the genital idea of…" Cue the awkward silence followed by a chorus of sudden giggles and whispers.

Now, how did you navigate that teaching minefield? Did you ignore it and keep going like a champ, desperately pretending you didn't just walk face-first into a verbal fumble? Or did you laugh it off, acknowledging the blunder by saying, "Well, that's one way to fix a typo in life!" Regardless, this moment became one of those legendary stories among your students, adding a layer of relatable humanity to your presence. The takeaway? Mistakes happen, and those laughing moments often create bonds stronger than any perfect lesson plan.

The importance of reflection is highlighted in research, which shows that taking the time to step back and consider what worked, what didn't, and how we felt throughout the process can lead to improved practices. But let's be honest: reflection isn't just a warm hug from the teaching gods—it often feels like standing in front of a mirror and realizing you've been wearing mismatched socks all day long. It can be uncomfortable, and sometimes it's easier to brush it off than to confront those moments head-on.

So, let's air out more grievances from our beloved teaching closets. How about the time you prepped your students for a big presentation, proudly displayed their fantastically crafted posters, only to realize that the poster board gloriously misspelled "chocolate" as "choclate"? Instead of letting your heart sink, do you dive into an impromptu lesson on the importance of proofreading, throwing some humor into the mix? "Looks like we have an emergency chocolate situation! Let's not let this poster create a candy crisis!"

These confessional moments serve a dual purpose: they provide a cathartic release and often expose the silly realities of the classroom. If we don't allow ourselves to engage in self-reflection, we miss the opportunity to recognize our growth and the ways in which those setbacks can illuminate our paths forward.

Here are some playful strategies to encourage your own reflection, ensuring that it becomes a regular practice rather than an afterthought:

1. Journaling: Keep a reflection journal where you jot down your triumphs, flops, and hilarious anecdotes from the day. Write about the days when you felt like you were nailing it and those moments when you wondered if all those coffee runs were worth it.

2. Feedback Loops: Create a safe space for your students to give feedback on your lessons (yes, it's okay to let them critique you!). "On a scale of 1 to 'I can't even,' how did today's lesson go?" Their insights can be both revealing and absolutely precious.

3. Celebrate the Wins: Have an end-of-week "praise parade" where you list out successes— big or small! Even if your only win was successfully keeping a straight face after an epic

student slip-up, congratulations! That's worth celebrating.

4. Peer Confessions: Create a buddy system with a fellow teacher where you share funny mishaps or discuss what's going well. Sometimes, just knowing you're not alone in this chaos can be the best medicine.

5. Reflective Questions: At the end of each week, ask yourself a few of these quick reflective questions: What brought me joy in teaching this week? What do I wish I could do differently? When did I find myself laughing out loud?

As we wrap up this chapter, let's remember that our teaching journey is lined with moments that both challenge and uplift us. Those seemingly awkward blunders, gut-busting stories, and heartfelt confessions are all part of what makes us exceptional educators.

Finding the joy in these reflections and experiences not only highlights our ability to grow but also helps us foster authentic relationships with our students. So take a step into the confessional—embrace the chaos, own the giggles, and don't forget to keep a sense of humor.

After all, in the theater of education, every misstep could lead to the most unforgettable scenes of laughter and learning.

Here are some inspiring scenarios for your chapter, "Reflection: The Teacher's Confessional," illustrating how these strategies changed a teacher's life or had a positive impact on their classroom:

SCENARIO 1:

THE POWER OF JOURNALING

After years of teaching, Mrs. Reynolds felt overwhelmed and disconnected. One day, she stumbled upon an old diary tucked away in her desk drawer—a relic from her college days. Inspired, she dusted it off and decided to start a reflection journal.

Each day after school, she jotted down her successes and hilarious mishaps: the time a student accidentally launched a paper airplane across the room during a serious discussion or when someone confused "geography" with "geography" (which led to a brief existential crisis).

As she filled the pages, something remarkable happened: she began to notice patterns in her teaching. The entries helped her appreciate the small wins, like when a previously shy student eagerly participated in a group project or when a difficult lesson suddenly clicked for the class.

Months later, armed with the insights from her journal, Mrs. Reynolds revamped her teaching strategies. This little ritual fostered a positive mindset and transformed her classroom environment. Her students picked up on her enthusiasm, sparking a newfound energy that made learning even more vibrant!

SCENARIO 2:
THE FEEDBACK LOOP REVELATION

Mr. Thompson, who often worried about how to connect with his students, decided to implement a feedback loop in his classroom after reading about its benefits. Each Friday, he would give out anonymous feedback forms asking students about their lessons: What worked? What didn't?

To his surprise, the students provided insights that were not only helpful but also chuckle-inducing. One student remarked, "The lesson was as engaging as watching paint dry... but the jokes made it bearable!" Mr. Thompson shared the feedback with the class, encouraging an open dialogue about what could improve.

Armed with their suggestions, he infused humor into his lessons and adapted his pace. By embracing their feedback, Mr. Thompson witnessed a remarkable change—students were not only paying closer attention but also becoming more actively engaged in discussions. This newfound approach fostered a supportive community where students felt their opinions mattered, ultimately boosting their confidence and participation!

SCENARIO 3:
CELEBRATING THE WINS

After a particularly trying term, Ms. Garcia decided that her classroom needed more positivity. She introduced "praise parades" every Friday, where students and teacher would gather and celebrate the week's accomplishments, no matter how small.

During one parade, a student shyly admitted, "I'm proud I didn't trip going up the stairs today!" Another chimed in with, "I actually finished my math homework without turning it into origami!" They laughed together, and the shared vulnerabilities created a tight-knit camaraderie.

As the weeks went on, celebrations filled with laughter transformed into an empowering ritual. Ms. Garcia noticed how her students began providing feedback to each other and cheering for their classmates during challenging tasks. The collective positivity spread throughout the classroom, leading to heightened motivation and a stronger bond among the group.

SCENARIO 4:
PEER CONFESSIONS AND COLLABORATIONS

Mr. Lee, feeling the burden of classroom management, hesitantly reached out to a fellow teacher for support. Together, they initiated "Peer Confessions," where each would share their funny mishaps along with strategies that worked—or didn't.

On one particular afternoon, Mr. Lee shared his most embarrassing moment of accidentally revealing that he once taught a history lesson on "Napoleon's War with the Pen" instead of "Napoleon's War with Spain." They both erupted into laughter, and surprisingly, this moment changed how Mr. Lee approached his students.

Replicating this lightheartedness in class, he invited his students to share their own goof-ups. Not only did it create a more relaxed atmosphere, but it also encouraged students to take risks in their learning. Before long, the class dynamic shifted; students learned to laugh at their mistakes and support one another, fostering resilience and a culture of shared growth.

SCENARIO 5:
REFLECTIVE QUESTIONS SPARKING TRANSFORMATION

Ms. Patel, feeling stagnant in her teaching routine, began a practice of asking herself reflective questions every Friday. "What brought me joy this week?" and "When did I laugh out loud?" became her guiding queries as she delved into the nuances of her week.

One week, she recognized that a spontaneous art project had ignited a spark in her classroom. Inspired, she decided to integrate more creativity into her syllabus. The following term, she implemented "Artistic Days," where students turned regular subject material into creative masterpieces.

The shift was remarkable! Students who had previously struggled in math began expressing their understanding through visual projects, and those shy about writing found their voices through poetry readings. Ms. Patel's reflection led to a transformative journey for her and her students, revitalizing their love for learning.

These scenarios illustrate how the strategies outlined in the chapter can lead to significant changes in a teacher's life or transform their classroom environment, highlighting the power of reflection, humor, and student engagement. Each teacher becomes more empowered, connecting more deeply with their students while enhancing their teaching practices.

Now, without further ado, let's transition to our final chapter, where we'll tackle self-care for teachers—because a tired, stressed teacher isn't half as fun and is certainly not equipped to handle the beautiful chaos of the classroom!

CHAPTER EIGHT

CELEBRATING GROWTH

From Rookie to Rock Star

Ladies and gentlemen, esteemed educators of all stripes, welcome to the First Annual Teacher Talent Show! Tonight, we're here to celebrate growth, learning, and the many comedic highs and lows encountered on the journey from rookie teacher to rock star! As we put on our glittering gowns (or favorite teacher T-shirts, no judgment here!), let's embrace the metaphor of the rising rock star, highlighting the achievements, gaffes, and joyful moments that have defined our careers.

Cue the Spotlight...

As we kick off this extravagant soirée, remember: every great rock star began somewhere—often with less-than-ideal performances. Think about the times when your lessons didn't go as planned, akin to a band fumbling through their first performance. Maybe you attempted a revolutionary method that turned into a complete flop. Remember that time when your STEM experiment blew up—literally? Or the time you prompted an entire class of students to attempt Shakespearean soliloquies, only to realize none of them quite understood what a "thou" was? Yet through these experiences, you've learned and evolved!

So, let's take a page from an awards ceremony and hand out some well-deserved accolades.

Announcing the First Award...

Best Unintentional Comedy goes to Ms. Johnson! For her unforgettable moment of accidentally calling a student "genital" while teaching about diagrams. Ms. Johnson, your ability to bring laughter into the classroom, even in the most awkward moments, is something we all aspire to!

Cue applause and laughter. Ms. Johnson blushes, knowing that incident will forever be a cherished story in her teaching lore.

Next Up...

The 'Oops' Award goes to Mr. Sanders! For that legendary moment when he forgot to mute himself during a class video call and treated his students to his entire grocery list. Who knew French bread and almond milk could spark such riveting discussions?

Mr. Sanders graciously accepts, reminding us all that even the best-laid plans can lead to humorous outcomes.

Research shows that celebrating small victories contributes to lasting motivation, and that's exactly the essence of this award show. Each of these comedic misadventures teaches resilience and creates a comradery that can uplift us during the tough weeks. Acknowledging both the big wins and the laughable blunders strips away the formalities that often surround professional achievements.

And Now, for the Most Inspirational Teacher Award...

This prestigious award goes to Mrs. Patel! For her phenomenal dedication to reaching out to every single student, even those who sometimes resemble furniture more than participants. Your "student shout-out" board has truly made a difference!

Mrs. Patel beams with pride as she remembers the countless times she bent down to greet a student only to find them snoozing on their desk. But she persisted, knowing that nurturing connections is what truly makes her classroom exceptional.

As we cap off this celebration of growth, let's reflect on what it truly means to journey from rookie to rock star. Along the way, we've triumphed and stumbled, shared laughter and lessons, and forged connections that will last a lifetime. Each moment of struggle or triumph contributes to who we are as educators—and, like any good concert, leaving us with unforgettable memories hugged in laughter.

Celebrate those victories in your everyday life, even the smallest ones. Did you manage to present a lesson without a single hiccup? Toss yourselves a mini-party! Did you catch a student understanding a complex concept? Give yourself a gold star! Always remember:

progress is not just about the milestones; it's also about celebrating the sometimes ridiculous path that brought you here.

So grab your imaginary microphone and take a bow, because whether you're teaching fractions, Shakespeare, or life lessons, you embody the spirit of a rock star. Let every dance break, pop quiz turned rap battle, and accidental blunder form a chorus harmonizing with your growth.

Now, as we conclude this inspiring yet humor-filled chapter, remember to keep celebrating each little forward step. Even if the journey from rookie to rock star feels daunting, recognize that each laugh, each lesson mastered, and even each blunder on your path is worthy of an encore! The spotlight is always on you, and together, we can keep the energy alive in our classrooms because teaching should always be a mix of joy, laughter, and a few delightful surprises along the way!

Here are some humorous and inspiring scenarios for your chapter, "Celebrating Growth: From Rookie to Rock Star," showcasing how a teacher's journey can encompass the challenges and triumphs of growth while adding a whimsical touch:

SCENARIO 1:

MS. JOHNSON'S COMEDY OF ERRORS

As Ms. Johnson stood before her class, ready to engage them with her lesson on the human body, she accidentally blurted out "genital" instead of "general." The room fell silent, and wide-eyed students exchanged glances as if she had just performed a magic trick gone terribly wrong.

Instead of crumbling under the awkwardness, Ms. Johnson seized the moment. "Well, folks, that's certainly not what I meant! Let's create a new genre of education: genital anatomy!" The classroom erupted with laughter, transforming a cringe-worthy mistake into a legendary moment.

Years later, her students still reminisce about that day, and Ms. Johnson wears her blooper badge with pride. "Remember, it's the unintentional comedy that turns a classroom into a community!" became her classroom motto, reminding her and her students that humor can turn even the most embarrassing mishaps into lasting memories.

SCENARIO 2:

MR. SANDERS' GROCERY LIST FIASCO

Mr. Sanders was having a normal day until he realized he forgot to mute himself during a virtual lesson. As his students tuned in, they were treated to an unintentionally riveting discussion about the merits of French bread. "Now, don't forget the almond milk with that! Oh, and we can't run out of ice cream," he said, completely unaware of the symphony of giggles emanating from his class.

When he eventually returned to his lesson, a field of raised hands greeted him. "Mr. Sanders, we need to know: what brand of ice cream do you recommend?" they chimed in, unable to resist the opportunity for free-range inquiry.

From that day forward, Mr. Sanders embraced a lighter approach to lessons. He introduced a "Snack Time Seminar" where students could bring their grocery lists (the educational kind) and share food-related fun facts. The accidental blunder became a cherished part of the syllabus, bridging education with laughter and snacks!

SCENARIO 3:

THE FURNITURE CONNECTION WITH MRS. PATEL

Mrs. Patel was determined to reach every student in her classroom, but one particularly sleepy student often resembled a piece of cozy furniture instead of an active participant. Every time she walked by, there he was—ideal for a soft seating arrangement but definitely not for discussions.

After weeks of effort, she decided to designate the plush couch in the corner as the "Chill Zone" for quiet reflection time. This allowed her sleepy student an opportunity to be comfortable while maintaining participation via tactile means (like soft squishy toys)—and surprisingly, it encouraged him to engage in the class discussions from the couch!

"Being a couch potato isn't just a position; it's a strategic approach to education!" became Mrs. Patel's mantra, and soon enough, her entire classroom atmosphere transformed into a space where every student's status—whether lively or laid-back—was celebrated. She often joked, "At least the furniture is learning too!"

SCENARIO 4:

CELEBRATING TINY VICTORIES

Recognizing the importance of celebrating even the tiniest triumphs, Ms. Rivera implemented "Victory Fridays" in her class. On these days, students would share their wins, big or small. From mastering long division to finally getting a compliment for their handwriting, everything was welcomed with open arms.

One Friday, a shy student named Charlie timidly shared, "I did my laundry without shrinking my favorite shirt!" The class burst into applause as if he had just won a Grammy. Ms. Rivera, impressed by his enthusiasm, proclaimed, "Next you'll be folding it like a pro! Only then can we talk about advancing to laundry skills level two!"

As the weeks went by, even the smallest accomplishments turned into elaborately celebrated events, creating an environment where students felt valued for their growth and effort. The notion that education should feel rewarding and fun blossomed into their culture, transforming the classroom into a vibrant community!

SCENARIO 5:

THE ROCK STAR DANCE-OFF

To cap off the year, Ms. Turner organized an end-of-term "Teacher Talent Show" where students could showcase their newfound skills, and, of course, her rock star moment was saved for last. She decided to use the finale to incorporate a dance-off inspired by her students' antics throughout the year.

As she busted out her best dancing moves—more interpretive than rhythmic—her students erupted into laughter. "Ms. Turner, I didn't know you had that in you!" shouted one eager student.

"What can I say? I'm not just a teacher; I'm a teacher-dancer—you can tell by my groovy grading style!" she quipped, trying to pivot into a questionable moonwalk. Everyone joined in on the laughter, and the dance-off instantly became an annual tradition.

Through playful performances, Ms. Turner fostered an environment where creativity flourished, and students felt empowered to express themselves fully. The teacher's show-stealing dance moves became part of the folklore of the school, reminding everyone that education can—and should—be a joyful performance!

These scenarios embody the spirit of reflection, growth, and humor found in teaching. They highlight the importance of using laughter to navigate the many milestones and challenges educators face on their journey from rookie to rock star, creating a sense of camaraderie and connection among teachers and students.

Thank you for joining this journey of laughter and learning. Here's to your ongoing success and the next chapter of your teaching life—and remember, rock stars never fade; they just keep playing!

FINALE

EMBRACE THE JOURNEY

A Teacher's Encore

As we draw the curtains on our journey through the vibrant world of teaching, it's fitting to take a moment for an encore—an opportunity to reflect on the chaos, the laughter, and the monumental growth that we, as educators, experience every day.

In the grand performance of teaching, every educator plays a vital role akin to that of a rock star, captivating their audience with a unique blend of knowledge, humor, and humanity. Just as musicians hone their craft through practice and performance, we too refine our methods with each lesson, learning from both our triumphs and mishaps.

So what does it truly mean to be a 'rock star' in the classroom? It means celebrating the small victories—the "aha!" moments when a student finally grasps a tricky concept or when laughter erupts from an unplanned classroom blunder. It encompasses the relentless spirit that transforms mistakes into learning opportunities, as Ms. Johnson did when she turned a slip of the tongue into a legendary moment that bound her class together in laughter.

Let us not forget the power of resilience. Each accidental baking soda eruption in Mrs. Jenkins's classroom or spontaneous TikTok moment with Mr. Thompson reminds us that the unexpected can often lead to the most memorable experiences. Just as rock stars must adapt and grow within the fickle bounds of their industry, embracing change and unpredictability is essential to our success as educators. It's about tapping into the joy of discovery, not just for our students, but for ourselves.

As we exit this stage of reflection, consider what you will carry forward. Will it be Ms. Patel's "Chill Zone" for students needing a little extra care, or the inspiring "Victory Fridays" implemented by Ms. Rivera, where every small win is celebrated? Remember, fostering an environment built on encouragement and humor yields not just engaged learners, but a tight-knit community ready to support each other.

As you step into your next school year, invite your inner rock star to shine. Hold tightly to your comedic mishaps; let them be the stories you share at faculty meetings. Embrace flexibility in your lesson planning and allow chaotic creativity to inform your teaching approach. After all, the unpredictability of teaching is its greatest charm—it's what keeps us on our toes and our hearts full.

Now, take one last bow, and remember this thrilling journey doesn't end here. Continue to forge connections, inspire growth, and most importantly, enjoy the audacious ride of teaching—because every moment, hilarious or heartwarming, deserves an encore. Here's to you—the educators, the rock stars of our classrooms. May your microphone never falter, your laughter resonate, and your passion continue to ignite the minds of future generations. Keep rocking on!

Thank you for joining this journey of laughter and learning. Here's to your ongoing success and the next chapter of your teaching life—and remember, rock stars never fade; they just keep playing!

www.ingramcontent.com/pod-product-compliance
Lightning Source LLC
Chambersburg PA
CBHW051223120626
46547CB00013B/1485